A differen[t] kind of me

CW00485316

Written by Pursher William
Illustrated By Nabeel Tahir

Hello, my name is Spike,

And I am autistic.

I go to nursery on my bike.

I zoom down the road

And run to my room

Oh, what a fright, oh, what a sight.

I walk into the room, and it is too bright.

From the ceiling to the floor,

It's brightness galore.

The displays, the trays.

And the light rays.

I climb on a chair.

At the light, I will stare,

Before flicking the switch,

Without even a twitch.

Then off I go to my favourite spot.

The corner with the pencils.

On the shelf way on top

My beloved pencils rescue the day.

Do not take them away, for my hands will sway.

They might land on the toys
or whatever's in sight.
With a crash and a bang,
And with all of my might.
I can make a big mess,
Or I might be distressed.
I could roll on the floor
With a scream; you cannot ignore it.

You call me once.
You call me twice.
I look not, and you
think it's not nice.
Please don't approach
me with an angry frown.

There are different ways you can help me calm down.
With a cuddle and a snuggle, you might stop all the trouble.
Patience you must bear. And you might have to stay near.
That's a great way to show me how much you care.

The noise! Oh, the noise,
sometimes too much to bear.
But I can always find safety
when I cover my ear.

I could sing, and I will do
my favourite tune.
A conversation with you I
am yet to begin.
You might give me a card, a
sign or a cue.
And from me, a few words
might come out of the blue.

Sometimes it's a struggle
For me to eat food,
But anything sensory,
To me tastes so good.

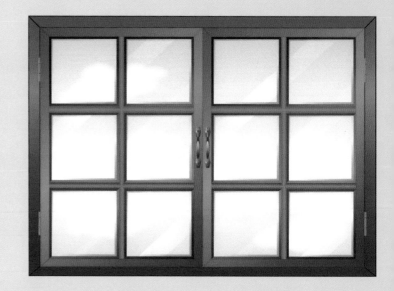

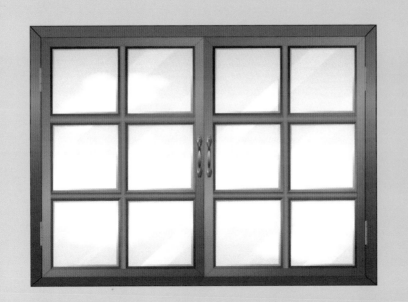

Play dough; I just love to eat.

To you, it may be a threat,

As for me,

It is such a treat.

On the carpet, I might fiddle.
I'm hardly found in the middle.
My own thing I might do,
Without looking at you.

In the garden.
I'm never steady,
As for running, I am always ready.

My hands might flap, and sometimes I clap.
I will tiptoe; I will spin.
And I won't hear when you say;
It's time to come in.

And when it's home time,
I love to hear the doorbell chime,
Ding dong, ding dong.
My day at nursery has been just fine.

For Gio – P. W.

Text copyright © 2023 by Pursher William

Illustration copyright © 2023 Nabeel Tahir

The right of Pursher William to be asserted as

the Author of this work has been asserted.

The End

Printed in Great Britain
by Amazon

40363248R00016